Also by Dan Gutman

My Weird School

My Weird School Daze

My Weirder School

My Weirdest School

The Baseball Card Adventure series

The Genius Files

Flashback Four #1: The Lincoln Project

Johnny Hangtime

Rappy the Raptor

My Weird School Fast Facts
Geography

Dan Gutman

Pictures by
Jim Paillot

HARPER
An Imprint of HarperCollinsPublishers

To Emma

Photograph credits: page 17: Vitalij Cerepok/EyeEm/Getty Images; 33: ullstein build/Getty Images; 36 © Bettmann/Corbis; 38: Hanquan Chen/Getty Images; 41 © Tull & Bruno Morandi/Corbis; 44: Jemina Virtanen/EyeEm/Getty Images; 47: Lizzie Shepherd/Getty Images; 51: Michele Falzone/Getty Images; 54 © Science Photo Library/Corbis; 56: Kevin Schafer/Getty Images; 61: Bill Curtsinger/National Geographic Creative; 65: Courtesy of NASA; 68: ullstein bild/Getty Images; 73: UniversalImagesGroup/Getty Images; 80 © Freeman Patterson/Masterfile/Corbis; 83: Image Source/Getty Images; 88 © Corbis; 89 © Guido Cozzi/Atlantide Phototravel/Atlantide Phototravel/Corbis; 90 © Richard Garvey-Williams/NIS/Minden Pictures/Corbis; 90 © Marc Serota/Corbis; 95: Martin Child/Getty Images; 98: Piriya Photography/Getty Images; 102: Danita Delimont/Getty Images; 104: Lola Akinmade Akerstrom/Getty Images; 111: Fotosearch/Getty Images; 112: Walter Bibikow/Getty Images; 114: SuperStock/Getty Images; 115: Philip and Karen Smith/Getty Images; 116 © Natural Selection David Spier/Design Pics/Corbis; 120: Courtesy of Bureau of Land Management File Photo; 121: mathieukor/Getty Images; 122: Courtesy of Hoag Levins/Hadrosaurus.com; 124: ullstein bild/Getty Images; 125: PhotoviewPlus/Getty Images; 148: John Elk/Getty Images; 155: Kylie McLaughlin/Getty Images; 155: Wesley Bocxe/Getty Images; 162: Samantha Marie Baranda/EyeEm/Getty Images

The author gratefully acknowledges the editorial contributions of Laurie Calkhoven.

My Weird School Fast Facts: Geography
Text copyright © 2016 by Dan Gutman
Illustrations copyright © 2016 by Jim Paillot
All rights reserved. Printed in the United States of America. No part of this book may be used or reproduced in any manner whatsoever without written permission except in the case of brief quotations embodied in critical articles and reviews. For information address HarperCollins Children's Books, a division of HarperCollins Publishers, 195 Broadway, New York, NY 10007.
www.harpercollinschildrens.com

ISBN 978-0-06-230620-3

22   BRR   10 9 8
❖
First Edition

Contents

The Beginning 1

Chapter 1: What Is Geography,
and Who Cares Anyway? 7

Chapter 2: Planet Earth 15

Chapter 3: The Continents 31

Chapter 4: Water 66

Chapter 5: Mountains, Deserts,
and Forests 85

Chapter 6: The Fifty United States 105

Chapter 7: Natural Disasters 135

The Ending 161

The Beginning

My name is Professor A.J. and I know everything there is to know about geography.

Geography is cool. Do you know why? Because it's all about exploding volcanoes that shoot red-hot lava up in the air, and earthquakes that swallow cars, and tornadoes that pick up cows and fling them across the highway, and hurricanes that rip trees out of the ground, and all kinds of cool stuff like that.

 Now, just wait a minute there, Arlo!

 Oh no! It's Andrea Young, this annoying girl in my class with curly brown hair. She calls me by my real name because she knows I don't like it.*

 Yes, my name is Andrea, and I know a lot about geography

---

*Don't bother reading Andrea's parts in this book. That's just the boring stuff.

too. Because I'm in the gifted and talented program at school.

But geography isn't just about natural disasters. Geographers explore and describe the earth and the people on it. They try to explain where things are, why they're there, how they change over time, and what all that has to do with the humans who live there. Geography is about our planet, the continents, and lakes, and rivers—

Zzzzzzzzz. Oh, sorry! I dozed off there for a minute. I couldn't help it, because Andrea is so boring.

But geography isn't boring. Did you

know that more than two-thirds of the earth's surface is made out of Jell-O? Did you know that when you reach the very top of Mount Everest, there's a McDonald's? Did you know that in Antarctica all the toilet bowls are upside down?

Arlo, you made all that up, and everybody knows it!

Well, yeah. But I do know a lot of *true* stuff about geography too. True *weird* stuff. Do you want to know what it is?

Well, I'm not going to tell you.

Okay, okay, I'll tell you. There's just one thing you have to do.

Turn the page.

Go ahead! Turn it! It's not like I'm going to turn it for you. I'm inside the book!

Yours truly,

Professor A.J.

(the professor of awesomeness)

 Andrea Young (I'm going to Harvard someday.)*

---

*Don't bother reading A.J.'s parts in this book. That's just the boring stuff.

What Is Geography, and Who Cares Anyway?

 I can handle the second part of this question. The answer is nobody. That's who cares about geography.

Okay, can we move on to the cool stuff, like exploding volcanoes and tornadoes that pick up cows and fling them across the highway? That's what I'd want to read about.

No, Arlo! Geography is really important! Why don't you go sit down over there and play with your little video games while I explain geography to the people?

 Sure! I love playing video games.

(Don't tell Andrea, but it's okay for you to skip this part of the book and go straight to the chapter about exploding volcanoes and flying cows.)

 Just ignore him. It's an attention-getting device.

It was the ancient Greeks who came up with the word "geography." It means "to write (or describe) the earth." They were the first geographers.

But for thousands of years, people didn't think much about geography. They had other things to worry about. You know what they worried about? They worried about whether or not they would have something to eat that day!

I can understand that. If I was living in a cave somewhere and a woolly mammoth was chasing me, I wouldn't be all that worried about describing the earth.

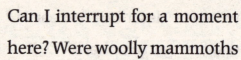
Can I interrupt for a moment here? Were woolly mammoths actually made out of wool? I don't think so. Because wool comes from sheep. I don't think that sheep would willingly give up their wool just to keep some mammoths warm. I bet that if there were woolly mammoths today, they would be made out of cotton or some synthetic fabric.

Just ignore Arlo. Anyway, geography didn't really take off until the Chinese started to use compasses as a navigation tool around the year AD 1000. A compass is a tool that helps you know which direction you're facing.

Suddenly, brave sailors were able to travel beyond their small area and see the world. In the early 1400s, a Chinese explorer named Cheng Ho set sail on seven voyages to the lands around the China Sea and the Indian Ocean.

Arlo, did you ever hear of Marco Polo?

Sure. Everybody knows about Marco Polo. That's a game we play in the pool during the summer. I am awesome at Marco Polo.

No, dumbhead! Marco Polo was an Italian merchant who traveled to Asia and came home to tell everyone about the mysteries of the Far East.

Oh yeah. I knew that. I was just yanking your chain. I know all about Marco Polo. He was that guy who went all

the way to China and brought pasta and ice cream back to Europe. That guy was cool.*

 Actually, most historians say there's no evidence of that. But even if Marco Polo didn't bring back pasta and ice cream, his travels started the Age of Exploration. Brave explorers

---

*Hey, how did Marco Polo keep the ice cream cold? Didn't it melt on the way home from China?

set off all over the world looking for gold, for new lands to conquer, and for spices.

They traveled the world looking for spices? Why didn't they just go to the supermarket? That's what my mom does whenever she needs spices.

They didn't have supermarkets back then! But from the fifteenth century to the seventeenth century, European explorers sailed all over the world. And after the printing press was invented in the 1400s, word got around that the world was an amazing place. Countries like the Netherlands,

Spain, and Great Britain started setting up colonies all over, including ones in North America that eventually became the United States.

Knowing about geography helped people spread themselves all over the world. It also helped people to understand their place in the world and who else lived in that world. *That's* what geography is all about!

Andrea thinks she is *so* smart because she knows a lot of stuff about geography. Why can't a truck full of geography books fall on her head?

Chapter 2

Planet Earth

In case you're a total dumbhead, let me just start by telling you that Earth is the name of the planet we live on. Duh! Everybody knows that. If you didn't know that, close this book right now and go to Walmart. They're having a sale on brains.

I'm sure everybody knows that the planet we live on is called Earth. But did you know that Earth is sort of like a giant rock that flies through space at sixty-seven thousand miles per hour?

Whoa! You better hold on tight so you don't fall off. Sixty-seven thousand miles per hour is way faster than my dad drives, even when he's going over the speed limit.

Like all the other planets in our solar system, Earth is constantly circling around the sun. Do you know how long it takes for the earth to go all the way around the sun just one time? 365 days. That's exactly one full year. What an amazing coincidence!

Satellite view of Earth and the moon

While Earth is constantly moving around the sun, it's also spinning around, like a top. If you've ever tried to rub your tummy and pat yourself on the head at the same time, you know how hard that can be. But Earth is very good at multitasking.

How fast is Earth spinning? About a thousand miles an hour.

Wow! No wonder stuff keeps sliding off my desk all the time.

 Actually, it doesn't *feel* like Earth is moving at *all*. It's sort of like when you're in a car driving down the highway at a constant speed. Close your eyes and you feel like you're staying in one place.

 Speaking of cars, do you know how a car's wheel turns around an axle? Well, the earth turns around this thing called an axis. The axis is not a *real* thing. It's an imaginary line that goes through the North Pole and the South Pole.

And by the way, the North Pole and the South Pole are imaginary things too. It's not like you go to the end of the earth and there's some big pole sticking out of the ground. That would be weird. The North and South Poles are just the points at the top and bottom of the earth.

Geography sure has a lot of imaginary stuff. I used to have an imaginary friend, but we got into an argument one time, and we haven't spoken to each other since.

Do you know how long it takes Earth to spin around its axis just once? Twenty-four hours, or exactly one day. That's why we have night and day, by the way. When your part of the earth is facing the sun, it's daytime. When it turns around so it's not facing the sun, you have night. And for people on the opposite side of the earth from you, your night is their day, and your day is their night.

Confused yet? Me too! But don't worry about it. Earth is going to keep on moving around the sun and spinning around its axis whether you know about it or not. And it's not like you're going to get tested on this stuff. At least not today.

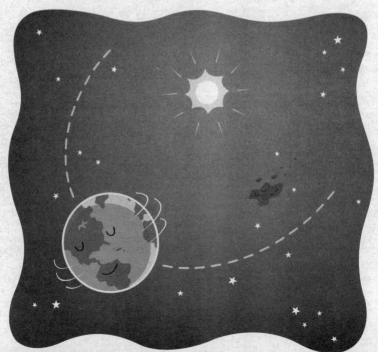

Speaking of imaginary lines, the equator is *another* one. It is right in the middle of the planet. Think of the equator as a belt that holds Earth's pants up. So North America would be the shirt, and South America would be the pants.

Everything above the equator is the earth's Northern Hemisphere, and everything south of the equator is the earth's Southern Hemisphere. A hemisphere is half of a sphere. Hemi means "half," and sphere means "a round object." So it has the perfect name!

If you were to drive a car all the way around the equator,

you would be driving 24,901 miles. You would also end up exactly where you started, so what would be the point of doing that? You might as well stay in one place.

And if you drove a car all the way around the equator, you would probably drown. Because most of the area around the equator is water. And cars can't drive through water.

Hey, do you know what the earth is made of?

It's made of earth, of course! Duh! It was a trick question.

Well, it's not quite as simple as that, Arlo. Earth is made mostly of rock, and it has three main layers. There's the crust, the thick center, and the core.

The crust is where we live. The earth's crust is between five and twenty-five miles thick. It's sort of like a pie crust, but you wouldn't want to eat the crust of the earth, because it would taste bad and you'd probably throw up. Nobody wants to eat earth.

Underneath the earth's crust is the mantle. It doesn't have anything to do with that baseball player

Mickey Mantle, even though it has the same name. But he was a great player, and he could bat both left-handed and right-handed. But not at the same time. That would be weird.

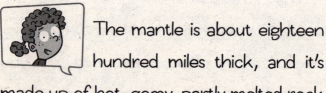

The mantle is about eighteen hundred miles thick, and it's made up of hot, gooey, partly melted rock called magma. Can you imagine how hot it must be if rocks are melting? Well, you don't have to. In the depths of the lower mantle, it's about 3,600°F.

And if you think *that's* hot, underneath the mantle is the

earth's core. The inner core can reach temperatures up to 12,600°F. That's so hot that when birds pick up worms, they have to use pot holders.

Okay, that's a joke.

How old is the earth? Nobody knows for sure. Well, it's not like the earth gets a birthday party every year, and we all blow out a certain number of candles. That would be a fire hazard anyway, because the earth is *really* old.

Scientists think that the planet is about 4.6 *billion* years old. Yes, I said billion. That's older than my grandmother, and she's pretty old.

 By the way, the moon is younger than the earth. Rocks brought back from the moon by astronauts in 1970 were found to be about 4 billion years old, and new research shows the oldest rocks from the moon to be about 4.4 billion years old.

 How do scientists know how old the earth and the moon are? Because they're really smart. Scientists use this thing called carbon dating to measure the ages of rocks.

Carbon dating isn't when two pieces of carbon go out on a date with each other. That would be weird. It's when you determine how old something is by measuring how much carbon is left in it. I know, it sounds complicated. That's because it is. If you want to find out how it works, grow up and become a scientist.

In the song "Imagine," John Lennon wrote, "Imagine there's no countries. It isn't hard to do." He was right.* The lines around the countries that you see on maps are more of those imaginary lines that geographers love so much. When you travel from one country to the next one, there isn't a big black line on the ground separating the two

---

*Except it should be "there *are* no countries."

countries. And if you go up into outer space and look down at Earth, you don't see countries. They all blend in with one another. It's too bad all the people in different countries can't get along and blend in with each other like their countries do on maps.

One last imaginary line is the international date line. This is the coolest of all the imaginary lines because it separates one day from the next day.

The international date line is in the middle of the Pacific Ocean, extending from the North Pole to the South Pole. So if you're on a boat that crosses that line heading east, you have to go *back* a day in the calendar, and you get to live yesterday one more time. And if you're on a boat that crosses the line heading west, you have to go *forward* one day in the calendar and miss a day of your life.

That's weird!

And if you happen to find yourself standing right *on* the international date line with one foot on either side of it, there's no telling *what* day you're in.

But you should really get back in the boat, because you're about to drown.

And that's all you need to know about the earth.

The Continents

Arlo, do you know what a continent is?

Sure. A continent is when you go to the bathroom in your pants.

 No, Arlo! You're thinking of *incontinence*!

 I knew that. I just thought it would be funny to talk about going to the bathroom in your pants in a book about geography.

Hey, speaking of going to the bathroom in your pants, can we talk about exploding volcanoes now?

 No! I'm going to try to put everything you just said out of my mind.

A continent is a really large landmass. There are seven of them on the earth. Here they are, in size order from biggest to smallest:

Asia, Africa, North America, South America, Antarctica, Europe, and Australia/Oceania.

It's hard to believe, but millions of years ago those seven continents were connected in one *huge* landmass called Pangæa. That means "all land."

Nobody knew that until 1912, when a German scientist named Alfred Wegener noticed that the coastlines of South America and Africa look like they could fit together, like the pieces of a jigsaw puzzle.

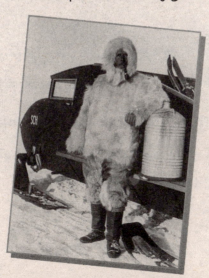

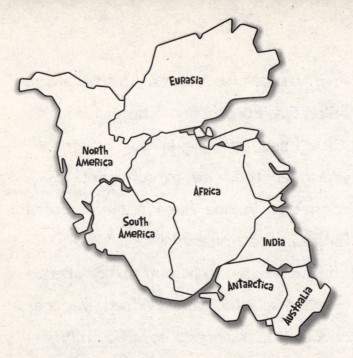

You can see them for yourself if you look at a map. Go ahead, we'll wait.

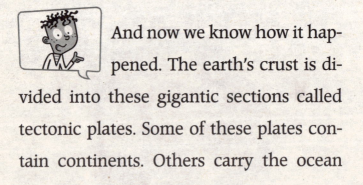

And now we know how it happened. The earth's crust is divided into these gigantic sections called tectonic plates. Some of these plates contain continents. Others carry the ocean floor. The plates float over the earth's bubbling, boiling, molten mantle sort of like rafts in a swimming pool.

 And believe it or not, these tectonic plates are moving right *now*, even as you read this. But don't worry. It's not like you're going to fall off the continent or anything. Tectonic plates can move only a few inches every year. They say that the continents move at about the same rate your fingernails grow.

That's just a weird comparison.

By the way, the Arctic is *not* a continent! Scientists used to think it was a huge landmass covered by ice, just like Antarctica. But in 1958, they discovered there's no landmass there. It's just floating ice.

How did they figure that out? Simple. A submarine went under the ice cap and came out the other side!

The USS *Nautilus* being prepared for its journey, 1958

Asia

 If you made a list of the biggest, the highest, and the lowest continents, Asia would be the winner. It's the biggest continent by far in square miles. It has the highest mountain in the world (Mount Everest). And it has the lowest point on the planet (the shores of the Dead Sea).

 Do you know how many people live in Asia? More than four *billion*. That's a lot of people! In fact, more people live in Asia than on all the other continents put together.

The Great Wall of China was begun in the eighth century BC. The Chinese wanted to defend their country from an invasion from the north. They worked on the wall for over two *thousand* years.

 Wow! My dad put up a wall in our basement. It only took a few days.

That's just silly, Arlo.

By the way, people will tell

you that the Great Wall is the only man-made object that can be seen from outer space. That's baloney. The wall is only thirty feet at its widest point. No way you're going to see that from space.

 In America, Stan is a guy's name. But in Central Asia, stan means "homeland." There are five countries there that end with "stan": Kazakhstan, Turkmenistan, Uzbekistan, Tajikistan, and Kyrgyzstan. And if you can spell any of them, you should get the Nobel Prize.

That's a prize they give out to people who can spell weird country names.

Did you ever wish you lived on an island? Well, you should go to Indonesia. This one country is made up of thirteen thousand islands! A lot of people must like to live on an island, because Indonesia is the fourth most-populated country in the world.

 My mom once told me a wise saying: no man is an island. That made no sense at all. No man is a toothbrush either. But we don't go around making up wise sayings about it.

 The Komodo dragon is a giant lizard that can only be found in Indonesia. It can grow to more

than ten feet and weigh over three hundred pounds. Komodo dragons eat all kinds of meat—including humans.

So maybe you don't want to go to Indonesia after all.

Europe

Do you know what they say when you go to the bathroom in France?

European! Get it? European? You're a-peein'?

That's horrible, Arlo.

I know. But did you know you could stand with one foot in Europe and one foot in Asia without even having to do a split? It's true.

Two countries—Russia and Turkey—are partly in Europe and partly in Asia. And there's one major city that is in *both* continents: Istanbul.

That's a good trivia question to ask your parents, by the way. I bet they won't get it right.

Unless, of course, you live in Istanbul.

Great Britain is a group of three countries in Europe and is also an island. To make things more confusing, the United Kingdom is made up of four countries—England, Scotland, and Wales, which are all part of Great Britain—and also Northern Ireland, which is not.

Almost half of the Netherlands is below sea level. That doesn't mean that the people of the Netherlands sit around underwater all day long. That would be weird. But thanks to a complicated system of dikes, canals, and pumping stations, they have managed to keep the water away from the land.

The word "Netherlands" actually means "low country."

It would be cool to hop on your bike anywhere in your country, ride for five minutes, and be in a different country. Well, there's only one place in the world where you could do that: Vatican City.

It's the smallest country in the world: one-fifth of a square mile. That's about the size of one hundred football fields.

Vatican City is in the middle of Rome,

Italy, and it's the seat of the Roman Catholic Church. Only about eight hundred people live there, but Vatican City has its own coins, stamps, and passports.

Africa

Here's another good question to ask your know-it-all parents: How many tigers are there in Africa?

The answer is . . . none!

It was a trick question. Tigers are native to *Asia*, not Africa. So nah-nah-nah boo-boo on your parents.

There are more than fifty countries in Africa, and the people there speak two thousand different languages. Well, *all* of them don't speak two thousand languages. That would be weird. Most of them probably only speak one or two languages. But you know what I mean.

Does your mom have a diamond ring or diamond earrings? They probably came from Africa. More than half of the world's diamonds come from there.

By the way, next to Arlo's head, a diamond is the hardest natural substance found on Earth. Diamonds are not just

46

used for rings and earrings. They're also used in saws and drills that can cut through granite.

 If you like to fly kites or ride dune buggies, you should go to Namibia. The rust-red sand dunes there are the highest in the world. The largest one is called Big Daddy, and it's more than a thousand feet high. Namibia would also be a good place to build sand castles.

The countries of Europe used to send people to Africa to establish colonies there the same way they had colonies in America. But by 1991, those colonies had all gained their independence, and most of them changed their names.

So if you look at a map of Africa from before the 1990s and compare it with a recent map, you'll see that most of the names of the countries are different. I guess the mapmakers were really happy, because everybody had to go out and buy new maps.

North America

 If you're reading this book, you probably live here, so you should know something about it. And if you're *not* reading this book, how do you even know I just wrote that?

 The highest point in North America is Mount Denali (also known as Mount McKinley). It's in Alaska, and it's 20,320 feet above sea level. That is *high*!

The lowest point in North America is Death Valley, California. It's 282 feet *below* sea level. We'll talk more about Death Valley later.

 If you look at a map, you'll see there's a lot of water between Siberia and Alaska. But thousands of years ago that water wasn't there. The first Americans actually *walked* here across that land bridge. That's how people spread across North America.

Ha, and you thought they took the train.

The Grand Canyon was carved by the Colorado River over millions of years. It's one of the Seven Wonders of the Natural World. Do you know how many dinosaur fossils have been found in the Grand Canyon?

None! That's because the canyon is so old that it's older than the dinosaurs!

Some people think Mexico is in South America. Those people are called dumbheads. Mexico is south of the United States of America, but that doesn't mean it's in South America!

Mexico is in North America. So are the countries of Central America: Belize, Guatemala, El Salvador, Honduras, Nicaragua, Costa Rica, and Panama. Central America is the strip of land that connects North and South America.

Mexico, Central America, and South America are sometimes called *Latin* America. That's weird, because hardly anybody there speaks Latin. In fact, hardly anybody *anywhere* speaks Latin.

 Greenland is the largest island in North America. It doesn't have the perfect name, because it's not very green. In fact, 80 percent of it is covered in ice. Only fifty-seven thousand people live in Greenland. That's less than the number of people who attend an average NFL game.

 Many scientists think the dinosaurs were wiped out

sixty-five million years ago when a comet slammed into North America and caused climate change. That comet left a huge crater,

Artist's rendering of the Chicxulub asteroid impact

and it's still there. It's in Chicxulub, on Mexico's Yucatán Peninsula.

And don't ask me how to pronounce Chicxulub.

Did you ever wonder why North America and South America are called America? I'll tell you why—they were named after an Italian explorer named Amerigo Vespucci.

So why weren't they named Vespucci? Because it would be weird to call our country the United States of Vespucci.

Speaking of South America...

Vespucci

South America

Like Europe and Asia, North and South America are really just one continent. They're connected by Central America, which is an isthmus.

Don't bother looking up "isthmus." I already did. An isthmus is a strip of land that connects two larger land areas.

The Amazon rainforest is the biggest tropical rainforest in the world. Over two and a half million square miles, it sits mostly in Brazil, Peru, and Colombia. The Amazon River, the second-longest river in the world, flows through the rainforest.

By the way, the *wettest* inhabited place on Earth is Buenaventura, Colombia.

 The highest waterfall in the world is Angel Falls in Venezuela. It is 3,212 feet high.

 Do you think there's a single place on Earth that has not been explored by humans? There could be.

Before 1911, no Westerner had ever seen or visited Machu Picchu. It's an ancient city in Peru built high in the mountains.

Australia, New Zealand, and Oceania

Did you ever hear of a continent called Oceania? I'll bet your parents never did either. But geographers now group Australia, New Zealand, Papua New Guinea, Tasmania, and thousands of islands in the South Pacific together into a continent they call Oceania.

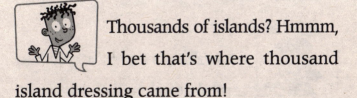

Thousands of islands? Hmmm, I bet that's where thousand island dressing came from!

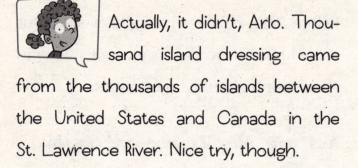 Actually, it didn't, Arlo. Thousand island dressing came from the thousands of islands between the United States and Canada in the St. Lawrence River. Nice try, though.

 Some of those thousands of islands in Oceania may someday be covered by the Pacific Ocean, if climate change leads to rising sea levels. Many people from the island country of Tuvalu have already moved to New Zealand, just in case.

 Australia has lots of interesting animals, like koalas, kangaroos, platypuses, and my personal favorite, the

Tasmanian devil. It's a meat-eating marsupial (that's an animal that carries its young in a pouch on the mother's belly) and it lives only in Tasmania—an island off Australia's southeastern coast.

The reason why Australia has a lot of plants and animals that are different is because it's so far away from Earth's other landmasses. In fact, Australia didn't have any cats, rabbits, or foxes until the Europeans brought them there.

Antarctica

Some days when I'm feeling sad, I want to run away to Antarctica and go live with the penguins. Penguins are cool. Their parents never yell at them. They don't have to do homework or go to school and learn stuff. Nobody tells the people in Antarctica that they're secretly in love with Andrea.

But if I actually went to Antarctica, I would be afraid. Because it's at the very bottom of the world. If you fall off the bottom, where do you go? Into outer space? I don't know. And I don't want to find out.

Do you know what the largest land animal is in Antarctica? If you guessed penguins, you're wrong! Penguins are sea animals.

The largest land animal in Antarctica is the wingless midge. It's an insect, and it's less than half an inch long.

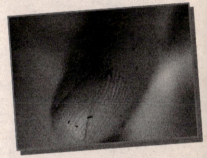

 Antarctica is where the South Pole would pop out if it was a real pole and not just some imaginary spot on the bottom of the world. But it is an imaginary place, so what's the point of talking about it? Santa Claus doesn't even live there.

Antarctica is the coldest continent on the planet. How cold is it? It's so cold that the birds pick up worms with gloves on.

That wasn't funny the first time, Arlo. But the truth is that it's so cold that there aren't any countries in Antarctica, and hardly any people.

The coldest temperature ever recorded on Earth was in Antarctica, of course. In July 1983, the temperature reached (are you ready for this?) 128 degrees below zero. Yes, that's *minus* 128 degrees. I feel sorry for the guy who had to go outside to check *that* thermometer.

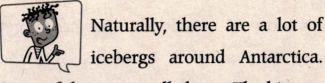 Naturally, there are a lot of icebergs around Antarctica. Some of them are really huge. The biggest iceberg ever seen in the waters around Antarctica measured 208 miles long and 60 miles wide. Wow! That's bigger than some countries.

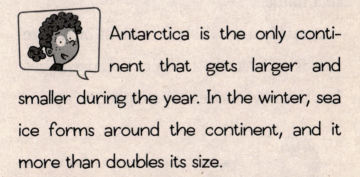 Antarctica is the only continent that gets larger and smaller during the year. In the winter, sea ice forms around the continent, and it more than doubles its size.

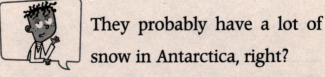 They probably have a lot of snow in Antarctica, right?
Wrong again! Snow doesn't form when

it's too cold outside. So they hardly get any snow at all in Antarctica. And the small amount of snow they *do* get never melts. It just builds up to form big sheets of ice. And you know what those sheets of ice are called?

Ice sheets! Duh! So they have the perfect name.

Actually, the whole continent of Antarctica is technically a desert because it gets less than two inches of precipitation a year.*

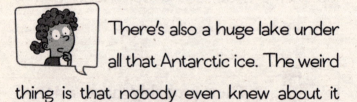

There's also a huge lake under all that Antarctic ice. The weird thing is that nobody even knew about it

---

*"Precipitation" is a fancy word for water that falls from the sky as snow, sleet, or hail.

Satellite image of Lake Vostok

until 1996, when scientists discovered it using radar. You probably wouldn't want to go swimming in Lake Vostok, though. It's two and a half miles under the ice cap.

Antarctica's ice cap holds 70 percent of the earth's freshwater. The other 30 percent is in my uncle's swimming pool.

Okay, I made that last part up. But my uncle *does* have a big pool.

If you ask me, Antarctica is cool. In more ways than one.

Water

Oceans

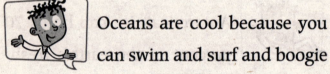

Oceans are cool because you can swim and surf and boogie board and collect seashells and buy cotton candy and go on rides.

One summer my family rented a beach house, and we went to the boardwalk and I ate so much candy and popcorn and salt-water taffy that I got sick to my stomach. It was the greatest day of my life.

 Arlo, eating junk food has *nothing* to do with the ocean. The important fast fact to know is that water covers more than two-thirds of the planet.

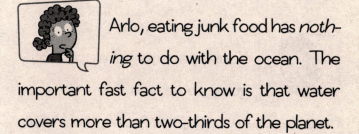 I knew that. But did you know this? The reason there are tides in the ocean is because of the *moon*. Isn't that weird? Why should the moon have anything to do with tides? Well, I'll tell you.

Just like we have gravity on Earth, the moon has gravity too. When the moon is overhead, the water in our oceans is pulled toward it. The water on Earth is attracted by the moon's gravity. So the water level in the oceans rises and falls every twelve hours.

Your parents are probably going to tell you there are four oceans—the Atlantic, the Pacific, the Indian, and the Arctic—but they're *wrong*. A few years ago, the International Hydrographic Organization (which is a fancy name for the people in charge of oceans) decided that there are really *five* oceans.

The fifth ocean is called the Southern Ocean. It includes the waters around Antarc-

An iceberg in the Southern Ocean

tica. Some people call it the Antarctic Ocean, just to make things even more confusing.

Actually, there is really just *one* big ocean. If you look at a globe, you'll see that all the oceans are connected in one way or another. Those bits of land we call continents just get in the way.

How deep are the oceans? On average, they're about twelve thousand feet deep. That might not mean much to you, but one mile is 5,280 feet. So the oceans are more than two miles deep. That's deep! Of course, some parts of the ocean are much deeper and some are more shallow. If there weren't shallow parts, you couldn't stand up in the ocean and dig your toes into the sandy bottom.

 The lowest point on Earth is a valley in the Pacific Ocean's Mariana Trench called Challenger Deep. It's thirty-six thousand feet deep! That's almost seven miles! Just to give you an idea of how big that is, if you picked up Mount Everest and dunked it into Challenger Deep, its peak would still be more than a mile underwater.

Of course, the tough part would be picking up Mount Everest in the first place.

The Pacific is the biggest of all the oceans by far. It covers almost a third of the earth's surface. It's fifteen times bigger than the United States, and it has tons of islands—twenty thousand to thirty thousand of them. Nobody really knows the exact number for sure. Some of them are tiny volcanic islands where nothing can grow, so no people live there.

It would be cool to live on an island with no people. But then, of course, if you lived there, it wouldn't be an island with no people anymore.

The Atlantic Ocean isn't nearly as big as the Pacific, but it's *getting* bigger. Because the tectonic plates in the earth are constantly moving, they're pushing the continents apart. The Atlantic is expanding at the rate of about one inch every year.

At some point, it will take longer to fly from the United States to Europe. It might be a few million years. But my dad told me you can save a lot of money by booking flights in advance.

 Here's another one to ask your parents: What is the longest mountain range on Earth?

Give up? It's the Mid-Atlantic Ridge. It's

an *underwater* mountain chain that runs down the middle of the Atlantic Ocean. The Mid-Atlantic Ridge is ten thousand miles long. It stretches all the way from the Arctic Ocean to the southern tip of Africa.

That's one mountain range that you probably don't want to ski down. It's really hard to ski underwater.

Of course, you could water-ski above it.

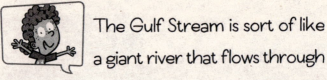 The Gulf Stream is sort of like a giant river that flows through the middle of the Atlantic Ocean. It's warmer than the rest of the ocean, and it moves from Florida up the East Coast and then all the way across the ocean to Europe. Without the Gulf Stream, northern Europe would be a lot colder than it is.

You'll never believe who mapped out and named the Gulf Stream.

It was Benjamin Franklin!

FRANKLIN

Lakes

Lakes are different from oceans, and not just because they're smaller. A lake is a body of water that is completely surrounded by land. Every continent has lakes—even Antarctica!

Do you like swimming in lakes? If so, you should go to Finland. It has more than 185,000 of them! That's a lot of lakes!

There have been lakes that were formed when a bunch of guys with bulldozers dug big holes in the ground. But mostly, the lakes on our planet were formed naturally. You may have noticed that most of North America's lakes are in the northern part of the continent. Like, there are zillions of lakes in Canada.

 About twenty thousand years ago, during the last Ice Age, glaciers from Canada started to slip and slide their way south. The moving ice cut into the ground, creating valleys and carrying rock away. When the glaciers started to melt, they turned into lakes and rivers. That's how America's Great Lakes were formed.

Can you name all five of the Great Lakes? Most people can't. Here's a little trick: Think of the word "HOMES." Each letter is the start of one of the Great Lakes: Huron, Ontario, Michigan, Erie, and Superior.

Or you could use the words "SHEMO," "ME OHS," or "SHO ME ."

Most lakes have freshwater—the kind that most plants, animals, and humans need to live. Of all the water on Earth, only about 2.5 percent of it is freshwater, and most of that is frozen or deep underground. That means we can use only 1 percent of the earth's water. That's kind of scary when you think about all the things we do with water. We drink it. We clean ourselves with it. We water our lawns and wash our cars with it. We fill our water balloons with it.

Do you and your friends ever have water balloon jousts? Water balloon jousting is the coolest sport ever. Especially when you joust on bikes.

One time, we were having a water balloon joust on the grassy field next to our school. My friend Alexia and I were the knights. We got on our bikes at opposite ends of the field—

Arlo, you're getting off topic again! The point is that we don't have a lot of freshwater. If you could put all Earth's water in a one-gallon jug, the freshwater available to humans would be about one tablespoon.

Thank you, Little Miss Know-It-All. But here's something you don't know: Lakes are a lot like pretzels. You can get them with or without salt.

The Dead Sea sits on the border of Israel and Jordan. It's not dead, and it's not a sea, so I don't know why it's called the Dead Sea. It's a lake, and it's almost six times saltier than an ocean. You don't want to drink the water, because it tastes really yucky.

Like most lakes, the Dead Sea is fed by rivers and streams that come down from the mountains around it. Those waters carry mineral salts. But there aren't any rivers or streams moving water *out* of the Dead Sea. The only water leaving is by evaporation. And in that hot, sunny climate, it evaporates like crazy. And do you know what water leaves behind when it evaporates? Salt, of course. *That's* why it's so salty.

 The coolest thing about the Dead Sea is that you can float in it even if you don't know how to swim. You couldn't drown if you tried! It's even hard to keep your legs on the bottom, because they keep wanting to float to the surface.

There's another salt lake right here in America. It's called the Great Salt Lake (which is the perfect name). It's in Utah.

Rivers

 Do you know why the Nile is the longest river in the world? Because it goes on for niles and niles and niles!

That's the oldest joke in the book. They probably told it in ancient Egypt. If you don't believe me, you're in denial. Or you're in the Nile. One or the other. Get it?

Are you quite finished with your little jokes, Arlo? People need to know that the Nile is 4,241 miles, and it runs through northeast Africa. It starts as two rivers—one in the mountains in East Africa and one in the tropics of central Africa—and flows into the Mediterranean Sea.

One of the greatest civilizations in the world, ancient Egypt, came to life on the banks of the Nile. Even today, more than nine out of ten Egyptians live within a few miles of the river.

The Amazon River in South America flows from the mountains of Peru through the rainforest in Brazil. It isn't as long as the Nile, but it's so wide that in some places it looks like a large lake. The Amazon carries more water than the world's next ten biggest rivers combined. Every second, it empties nearly fifty-seven *million* gallons of water into the Atlantic Ocean!

 Quick! What's the longest river in the United States? No, it's not the Mississippi! Nice try!

The longest river in the United States is the Missouri, which is 2,540 miles long. That's about two hundred miles longer than the Mississippi.

Chapter 5

Mountains, Deserts, and Forests

Mountains

 Why do we have mountains? Because if we didn't, mountain climbing would be *really* boring.*

---

*It's almost time for the chapter on natural disasters! I can't wait!

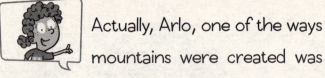 Actually, Arlo, one of the ways mountains were created was by those moving tectonic plates in the earth that we talked about earlier. When two plates carrying landmasses push against each other, *crash! Bang! Boom!* A mountain range is born.

For example, the Ural Mountains in Russia mark the spot where Europe and Asia crashed into each other.

But the biggest, most dramatic head-on collision of two plates happened when India crashed into Asia and created the world's tallest mountain range: the Himalayas.

 I know the tallest peak in the Himalayas: Mount Everest.

It's a whopping 24,035 feet above sea level, and it's still growing! The tectonic plates are still moving, and some scientists say Everest grows as much as 2.4 inches every year. Other scientists say it's just growing about 4 millimeters a year—less than a quarter of an inch. I say those scientists should make up their minds.

George Mallory from England was one of many mountain climbers who wanted to be the first to reach the summit of Mount Everest. When reporters asked him why he wanted to do it, he replied, "Because it's there." That guy was cool.

Unfortunately, he never made it. George

Mallory died eight hundred feet from the top of Mount Everest in 1924. He was just thirty-seven.

Tenzing Norgay and Edmund Hillary

Everest wasn't conquered until twenty-nine years later, by Edmund Hillary and Tenzing Norgay.

Mount Everest is the highest mountain. But it's *not* the tallest mountain.

Huh?

Some mountains are *underwater*. The tallest mountain on Earth is Mauna Kea, a volcano on the island of Hawaii. The base of Mauna Kea is at the bottom of the Pa-

88

cific Ocean, so the summit only rises 13,796 feet above sea level. But Mauna Kea is 33,000  feet tall, much higher than Mount Everest.

I wonder if Mount Everest is jealous.

 Do you know how an underwater mountain gets formed? Sometimes those tectonic plates carrying the ocean floor move *away* from each other, and the hot, bubbling, molten magma from under the earth's crust bubbles up and makes huge underwater mountains.

You probably don't want to go mountain climbing on an underwater mountain. Falling off the mountain wouldn't be much of a risk, but you might drown.

Many mountain climbers make it their goal to climb the Seven Summits: the highest points on each of the seven continents. The youngest person ever to climb the Seven Summits was Jordan Romero from California. He was just nine when he reached the top of Mount Kilimanjaro in Africa, and thirteen when he climbed Mount Everest.

Mount Kilimanjaro. Romero also climbed Mount Elbrus, Mount Aconcagua, Denali, Mount Carstensz Pyramid, Mount Everest, and Vinson Massif.

Scientists believe that over millions of years, the mountains we see today will fade away. They'll sink under their own weight, and rock will be worn away by rain, wind, and snow.

If Earth's crust stops moving and the mountains disappear, it will be sad. Especially for snowboarders and skiers.

In 2005, scientists discovered a mountain in Mozambique, Africa, that most of the world didn't know existed: Mount Mabu. They didn't go to Africa to find it. They found it on Google Earth!

So maybe there are more mountains

out there waiting to be discovered. Maybe *you* will be the person to discover one.

Deserts

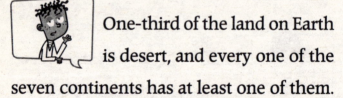

One-third of the land on Earth is desert, and every one of the seven continents has at least one of them.

Do you know the difference between a desert and a dessert? A desert is any place that gets less than ten inches of rain or snow a year. A dessert is a tasty treat you have at the end of a meal. If I had the choice between being stranded in a desert or stranded in a dessert, I would definitely choose the dessert. At least you get something to eat.

 The biggest desert in the world is . . . the Sahara in North Africa, right?

Wrong! According to the definition of a desert, the largest one in the world is in Antarctica! I'll bet your parents don't know that.

The Sahara is the biggest *sub-tropical* desert. It stretches across eleven countries. But it's not the sandy desert you're thinking of. It's only 30 percent sand. The rest is rocky and mountainous.

The Arabian Desert on the Arabian Peninsula is the world's largest sand desert. There's another desert on the Arabian Peninsula called the

Empty Quarter that is nothing but sand dunes. It's about the size of France!

The Gobi Desert in China and Mongolia and the Patagonian desert in Argentina are cold-winter deserts. In the Gobi, the temperature can get as hot as 113°F during the day and as low as −40°F at night.

So if you go there, bring lots of sunscreen *and* your winter coat.

The reason why some deserts get so little rain is because of the "rain shadow effect." When a mountain range stops moisture from reaching an area, the land is in the mountain's "rain shadow."

For example, the Himalayan Mountains are right next to the Gobi Desert, and they prevent rainfall from reaching it. So one side of the Himalayas gets up to six hundred inches of rain a year, and the other side gets less than ten inches a year.

The air is so dry in subtropical deserts that rain can evaporate before it even reaches the ground! Most animals can't survive in these hot, dry deserts. But camels, snakes, and scorpions can. None of them need much water, and they're more active at night when it's cooler. Snakes have scaly skins that stop them from drying out, and they can go a long time without food. Desert plants have leaves that hold on to moisture.

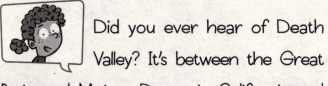 Did you ever hear of Death Valley? It's between the Great Basin and Mojave Desert in California and Nevada. Death Valley is one of the hottest, driest places on Earth because it's in the rain shadow of *two* mountain ranges: the Pacific Coastal and the Sierra Nevada ranges.

Badwater Basin in Death Valley is the lowest point in North America: 282 feet below sea level.

The hottest temperature ever recorded on Earth was in Death Valley's Furnace Creek on July 10, 1913. It was 134°F. Ouch! I'll never complain about the heat again! No wonder they named it Death Valley.

The *average* temperature in Death Valley in July is 116°F. People actually go there on vacation. Nobody knows why.

But Death Valley isn't the driest place on Earth. That honor goes to the Atacama Desert in South America. It gets just one *millimeter* of rain every year. In fact, there are parts of the Atacama where not one drop of rain has *ever* been recorded! It is so much like another world that NASA went there to test the Mars rover.

Forests and Trees

Trees can breathe!

They're like the earth's giant air conditioners, because trees take carbon dioxide and other pollutants out of the atmosphere and turn them into oxygen.

One tree can absorb almost fifty pounds of carbon dioxide in a year. So in its lifetime, that tree will suck up as much CO_2 as an average car would produce if it was driven around the world.

Trees are old!

The world's oldest tree is a bristlecone pine tree in the White Mountains in California. It's 5,063 years old. I would tell you exactly where it is, but the locations of the world's tallest and oldest trees are kept secret. Otherwise, tourists might damage them looking for souvenirs to bring home.

There's a colony of quaking aspen trees in Utah with a root system called Pando that is eighty thousand years old. It's the oldest living organism on the planet. And because these trees are connected by a single massive root system, it is also the world's heaviest known organism, at 6,600 tons.

 They say everything is bigger in Texas, but the boreal forest in Russia covers an area that is more than seventeen times the size of Texas. Wow!

 Paper is made from trees, of course. So is furniture and anything made from wood. In fact, more than five thousand things are manufactured from trees.

Trees are tall!

 The redwood trees in Northern California can grow more than 350 feet

tall. That's about the average size of a skyscraper.

 Did you know that aspirin was originally developed from willow bark? Actually, we get lots of good stuff from trees. In fact, more than 25 percent of the medicines we use come from rainforest plants.

Trees are dangerous!

 The bark of the manchineel tree is covered in sap that can make you go blind if it gets in your eyes. Just standing under it will cause blisters on your skin if the sap drips on you. And if you eat the fruit of this tree, you could die! Eek! It's found in the Caribbean and Gulf of Mexico.

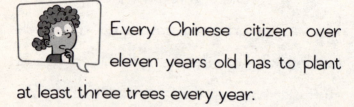

Every Chinese citizen over eleven years old has to plant at least three trees every year.

There's a hotel in Sweden called Treehotel that has all its rooms up in the trees.

The Fifty United States

 The United States of America is a weird place to live! Here are fifty-one reasons why....

Alabama

 Scratch Ankle, Smuteye, and Chigger Hill are all towns in Alabama.

Alaska

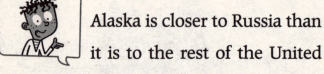

Alaska is closer to Russia than it is to the rest of the United States. In one place, Russia is two and a half miles away!

Arizona

The Painted Desert isn't painted, and the Petrified Forest isn't scared.

The Painted Desert was named by Spanish explorers, who marveled at the colors of the landscape. The Petrified Forest was named for its large deposits of petrified wood.

Arkansas

 Arkansas has the only diamond mine in North America. If you find a diamond there, you can keep it!

California

California is home to the tallest waterfalls in the country (Yosemite Falls); the lowest, driest, and hottest point (Death Valley); and the tallest, biggest, and oldest trees in the world. The world's tallest living tree, Hyperion, is a 379-foot redwood.

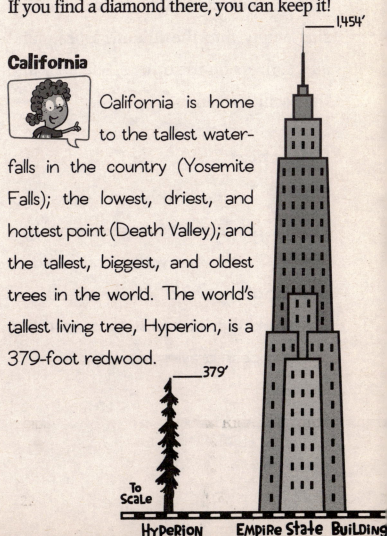

Colorado

A land formation called the Continental Divide runs through Colorado. All the rivers on one side empty into the Atlantic Ocean, and all the rivers on the other side empty into the Pacific Ocean.

Connecticut

Fifteen thousand years ago, Connecticut was covered by a glacier. So it's very young compared to the rest of the world.

Oh, and they have a state insect there: the European praying mantis.

Delaware

 There are parts of Delaware that are only nine miles wide. Delaware is the only state without any national parks, seashores, historic sites, battlefields, memorials, or monuments.

And, by the way, one of the state colors of Delaware is buff.

Florida

 Florida is the lightning capital of the world. Sea breezes from the Gulf of Mexico and the Atlantic Ocean collide over the warm Florida peninsula. That means lots of thunderstorms and lightning.

Georgia

Marshall Forest in Rome is the only natural forest within a city limits in the United States.

The large-flowered skullcap, an endangered plant found in Marshall Forest

Hawaii

Hawaii is in two places at once. It's part of the United States, of course. But geographically, it's part of the Polynesian cultural region of Oceania.

It is made of eight big islands and more than a hundred small ones. They were formed when volcanoes grew over a hot spot—a place where magma bursts through the tectonic plates. Some Hawaiian volcanoes continue to erupt from time to time. Every time Mauna Loa erupts, the Big Island of Hawaii gets a little bit bigger.

Idaho

Craters of the Moon National Monument in central Idaho is so much like the moon that NASA used it to train astronauts for the Apollo missions.

Illinois

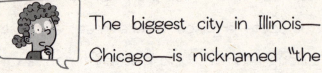

The biggest city in Illinois—Chicago—is nicknamed "the Windy City," but it's not because it is so windy. A New York City newspaper editor gave the city its nickname because he thought Chicagoans bragged too much about the Chicago World's Fair of 1893.

Indiana

Indiana is famous for its beautiful limestone. The Empire State Building, Rockefeller Center, the Pentagon, the United States Treasury, a dozen other government buildings in

Washington, DC, and fourteen state capitols were built using Indiana limestone.

Iowa

Iowa is the only state whose name starts with two vowels. Hogs outnumber humans four to one there.

Seventy-four million years ago, an asteroid or comet struck the earth near Mansfield. And it's still there. The crater it created is hidden below the surface and stretches twenty-four miles in diameter.

Kansas

Kansas is flatter than a pancake. Scientists actually compared its land with a pancake from IHOP. Maybe that's why farmland covers more than 88 percent of the state.

Kentucky

Mammoth Cave in the Green River valley is the longest known cave system in the world. Nearly four hundred miles of underground passages, lakes, rivers, and waterfalls have been explored, but there's still more to go.

Louisiana

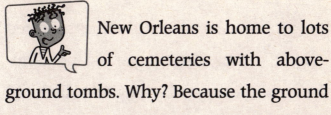 New Orleans is home to lots of cemeteries with above-ground tombs. Why? Because the ground is too wet to bury people underground.

Maine

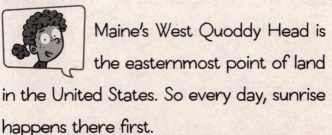 Maine's West Quoddy Head is the easternmost point of land in the United States. So every day, sunrise happens there first.

Maryland

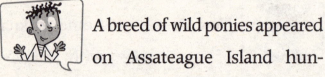

A breed of wild ponies appeared on Assateague Island hundreds of years ago. They're called the Chincoteague ponies. Some people believe they are survivors of wrecked Spanish ships. Or maybe they're descendants of domestic horses transported to the island in the 1600s. Nobody knows for sure. But they are still there today.

Massachusetts

 In Webster, there is the place in the United States with the longest name. It is Lake Chargoggagoggmanchauggagoggchaubunagungamaugg. I didn't make that up. It's a Nipmuc word that means "Englishmen at Manchaug at the Fishing Place at the Boundary." But because of an article by *Webster Times* editor Larry Daly, the translation more people know is "You fish on your side; I fish on my side; nobody fishes in the middle."

Michigan

 Four of the five Great Lakes touch Michigan. If you go to

any point in the state, you'll never be more than eighty-five miles from one of the Great Lakes.

Minnesota

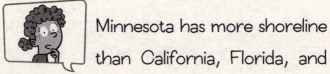
Minnesota has more shoreline than California, Florida, and Hawaii combined. It has ninety thousand miles altogether.

And in case you were wondering, the original name of the city of St. Paul was Pig's Eye Landing.

Mississippi

Mississippi is home to the world's largest cactus planta-

tion, in Edwards. It is also home to the largest pecan nursery (Lumberton), the cotton capital of the world (Greenwood), the catfish capital of the world (Belzoni), and the sweet potato capital of the world (Vardaman).

Missouri

Missouri ties with Tennessee as the most neighborly state in the union. Both of them are bordered by eight states.

Montana

Montana means "mountainous" in Spanish. There are more cattle than people in this state. The largest snowflake ever seen was in Fort Keogh. It was fifteen inches in diameter.

Nebraska

 The Nebraska National Forest was entirely planted by people.

Nevada

 Nevada is the most mountainous state in the country. It has 315 counted mountain ranges.

Sand Mountain is called "the singing sand dune." If you go there, you can hear weird noises caused by the grains of sand rubbing against each other.

New Hampshire

The White Mountains are where you can find the highest peak in the Northeast: Mount Washington. It's 6,288 feet high. But who's counting?

The White Mountains are known for their intense winter storms. The highest wind speed ever recorded was on Mount Washington on April 12, 1934. It was clocked at 231 miles per hour.

New Jersey

 In 1858, the first nearly complete dinosaur skeleton found in North America was dug up in Haddonfield. It was named hadrosaurus, but everybody calls it Haddy. In the middle of town, they have a big statue of it.

New Mexico

 Carlsbad Caverns are the deepest limestone caves in the United States. You could fit six football fields into the largest chamber, which is called the Big Room. Playing football in a cave would be cool.

Every night between March and October, thousands of bats fly out of the caves and then return in the morning.

New York

Glaciers carved out the Great Lakes—two of which sit on New York's border with Canada (Lake Ontario and Lake Erie). Glaciers are also responsible for the Finger Lakes, a group of eleven long, narrow lakes that resemble fingers (so they have the perfect name).

North Carolina

The Wright brothers were not from North Carolina. They lived in Ohio. But they brought their

airplane to Kitty Hawk in the Outer Banks of North Carolina because the National Weather Service said it had strong, steady winds (for flying) and lots of soft sand (for landing).

North Dakota

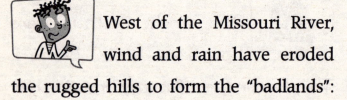 West of the Missouri River, wind and rain have eroded the rugged hills to form the "badlands":

rock formations like canyons, gullies, ravines, buttes, and mesas that are nearly impossible to get through on foot.

Ohio

 Johnny Appleseed was a real person who spent most of his life planting apple trees in the Ohio River valley. He also gave seeds and seedlings to everyone he met.

Oklahoma

Sixty-seven Native American tribes have lived in Oklahoma. Most of them *walked* there when the government took their land and forced them onto reservations. The journey became known as the Trail of Tears.

A Choctaw chief gave the state its name: "okla" (people) and "homa" (red).

Oregon

Crater Lake is 1,943 feet deep—the deepest lake in the United States. It's inside a dormant volcano. After the volcano erupted 7,700 years ago, the upper half collapsed into an empty magma chamber.

Pennsylvania

Pennsylvania is where all the pencils in the world are made. Okay, that's a total lie. But this is true: The state's best known animal is Punxsutawney Phil, a groundhog. On Groundhog Day (February 2) every year, if he sees his shadow, that means we'll have six more weeks of winter.

Rhode Island

Rhode Island is the smallest state. In fact, it's smaller than some counties in other states. No place in Rhode Island is more than a half-hour drive from the ocean or bay.

South Carolina

Cotton was king in South Carolina until a beetle called the boll weevil destroyed the crops in the 1920s and farmers were forced to plant other crops.

South Dakota

Like North Dakota, South Dakota has an area of badlands. Fossils of ancient mammals like rhinos, horses, and saber-toothed cats have been found there. The badlands erode by about one inch per year.

Tennessee

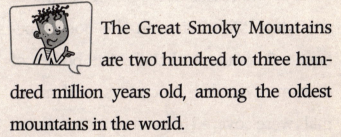

The Great Smoky Mountains are two hundred to three hundred million years old, among the oldest mountains in the world.

Texas

They say everything is bigger in Texas. The state is bigger than most countries, including every country in Europe except Russia. Texans fought Mexico for independence and won in 1836. It was its own country until 1845, when it became the twenty-eighth state.

Utah

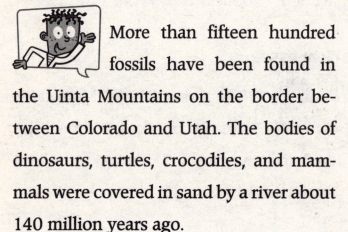

More than fifteen hundred fossils have been found in the Uinta Mountains on the border between Colorado and Utah. The bodies of dinosaurs, turtles, crocodiles, and mammals were covered in sand by a river about 140 million years ago.

Vermont

Samuel de Champlain first explored the area

of present-day Vermont, and he named the famous Lake Champlain after himself.

Virginia

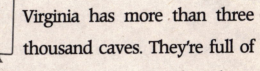

Virginia has more than three thousand caves. They're full of stalactites (which grow downward) and stalagmites (which grow upward). Water deposits minerals on them, so they're growing—slowly. It takes about 120 years to add a cubic inch to the stalactites and stalagmites.

Washington

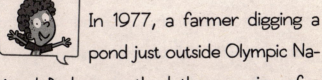

In 1977, a farmer digging a pond just outside Olympic National Park unearthed the remains of a mastodon with a spear point poking out of one of its ribs.

West Virginia

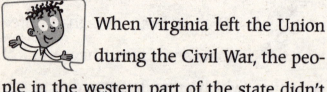

When Virginia left the Union during the Civil War, the people in the western part of the state didn't want to leave. So they formed their own state: West Virginia!

Wisconsin

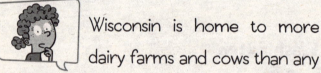

Wisconsin is home to more dairy farms and cows than any other state. Cow's milk is used to make cheese, which led to the nickname for people who live in Wisconsin: Cheeseheads.

Wyoming

Yellowstone National Park has more geysers than any other place on Earth. Do you know what a geyser is? Those are places where heated water and steam shoot out of the ground.

The large geyser that erupts more frequently than all the others is called "Old Faithful."

Washington, DC

At first, New York City was the capital of the United States. Then the capital was moved to Philadelphia. And then it was moved to Washington, DC.

Do you know why Washington was chosen? In 1790, it was decided that the capital should be right in the middle of the North and the South. Land was donated by Maryland and Virginia.

Natural Disasters

Well, it's about time!

It's about time to talk about titanic tornadoes and enormous earthquakes and horrific hurricanes and terrible tsunamis. I've been waiting the whole book for this moment.

Natural disasters are cool. Unless, of course, you happen to be in the middle of one. Then I suppose, it's not so cool.

Let's start with . . .

Earthquakes

Did you know there are about half a million earthquakes every year? It's true. Most of them are hardly noticed by anybody. The others, well, those are the cool ones.

It's hard to name the biggest earthquake of all, but one of the deadliest ones took place in Shaanxi, China, on January 23, 1556. It just about wiped out an area of 520 square miles.

Sixty-six-foot cracks opened up in the ground. Mountains and rivers actually changed places. Hundreds of buildings were destroyed. 830,000 people died. That's nearly a *million* people. And people felt the tremors from that earthquake in ninety-seven countries around the world.

Why do we have earthquakes? In ancient Greece, they believed earthquakes were caused by the god of the sea, Poseidon. When he was angry, he'd hit the ground with his trident and set off a quake.*

Weird, right? But in old-time Japan, they believed that earthquakes were caused by a giant catfish named Namazu.

Now, of course, thanks to science,

---

*What a bunch of dumbheads those ancient Greeks were!

we know that earthquakes are caused when elephants go bowling.

Okay, that's a joke.

Earthquakes are caused when the earth's tectonic plates grind against each other. The place where two plates meet is called a "fault." When the plates move, energy is built up. It needs to go somewhere, so it gets released along a fault. That energy radiates in all directions in what scientists call "seismic waves."

The strength of these waves can be measured using the Richter scale. It has the perfect name, because it was devised by a guy named Charles Richter in 1935.

The higher the number on the Richter scale, the bigger the earthquake. A medium-size earthquake might measure 5. Each whole number is an increase of ten times the previous number. So a 6.2 earthquake is ten times bigger than a 5.2 earthquake.

The strongest earthquake ever measured was in Chile in 1960—it measured 9.5 on the Richter scale. You wouldn't want to be in Chile in 1960.

You also wouldn't want to be in San Francisco in 1906. That

was before they had the Richter scale, but most of the city was destroyed after an earthquake. Almost all the damage was done by fire after the earthquake cracked the gas pipes. San Francisco burned for three days and nights.

Between December 1811 and February 1812, three big earthquakes hit the Midwest. They shook the earth so much that parts of the Mississippi River flowed *backward.* That must have been weird!

The first quake, in Arkansas, could be felt as far away as New York City. The third one destroyed the town of New Madrid, Missouri.

Almost all the world's earthquakes happen on the edges of the Pacific Ocean. The area is called the Ring of Fire, which is a pretty good name because most of the world's active volcanoes are there too. Japan and California are both in the Ring of Fire.

Speaking of California, that's where the famous San Andreas Fault is. The tectonic plates there are moving about one and a half inches every year. Eventually San Francisco and Los Angeles will come together to make one really big place. But you don't have to worry. It will take fifteen million years for the two cities to meet.

Some scientists think animals can detect an earthquake before it happens by feeling weak tremors we can't sense. Other scientists think that animals detect electrical signals that are set off by the movement of underground rocks just before an earthquake hits.

 The average earthquake lasts about a minute. But it can be so powerful that it can release hundreds of times more energy than the atomic bomb that was dropped on Hiroshima in Japan at the end of World War II.

Earthquakes can also set off landslides and avalanches,

which would be really cool if they didn't cause so much damage. The same goes for when the center of the earthquake (called the epicenter) is located in the ocean. That's when you get a tsunami.

Tsunamis

Tsunami is a Japanese word that means "harbor wave." That's an understatement!

In December 2004, there was a 9.0 earthquake in the Indian Ocean. It set off a tsunami that hit Thailand, Sri Lanka, parts of Indonesia, and the coast of Somalia, in Africa. More than two hundred thousand people were killed, in fourteen countries. More than a million and a half people were left homeless.

This is a natural disaster you can see with your own eyes. With your parents' permission, go on YouTube and search for "2004 tsunami."

Here's what happens with a tsunami: An earthquake occurs on the ocean floor. The shock waves ripple through the water and create huge waves. They might not be noticed in the middle of the ocean because the waves are very wide, but they move really fast. The closer they get to the coastline, the steeper those waves get. Before you know it, there's a 130-foot wall of water heading right for you.

A tsunami can also be triggered by a landslide that drops into the sea. And a volcano can trigger a tsunami if its eruption is so huge it blows itself apart. Yikes!

Speaking of volcanoes...

Volcanoes

A volcano occurs when there's a rupture in the crust of the earth and hot lava, ash, rocks, and gases escape from deep below the surface. During one eruption in the Philippines in 1991, ash flew twenty-one miles up in the air!

 The biggest volcanic eruption in recorded history happened when Indonesia's Tambora volcano suddenly let loose in 1815. People heard the explosion over a thousand miles away. It caused tsunamis, and gas and ash filled the sky for so long that 1816 was known as "the year without a summer." Crops stopped growing, causing a huge famine. As many as one hundred thousand people died worldwide.

 When hot, liquid rock is below the surface of the earth, it's called magma. Once magma reaches the surface and starts to cool, it's called lava. But even lava can be as hot as 2,120°F.

 As it cools, lava hardens and forms new rock. With enough lava, you get an island, or a whole chain of them—like the Hawaiian Islands.

 In 2015, the Calbuco volcano in southern Chile erupted. It spewed ash miles up into the sky and set off lightning bolts. They had to cancel

flights in and out of most of the countries of South America.

The sixty tallest volcanoes on Earth are in South America. The highest one is Chimborazo in Ecuador. It's 20,700 feet above sea level.

Some volcanoes are extinct, which means they're no longer active. Other volcanoes will go for many years without an eruption. These are called dormant volcanoes. That basically means they're asleep.

But they can wake up anytime. The most dangerous volcanoes are those sleeping mountains that haven't erupted in centuries. People forget about them. They start building houses and farming nearby. And then—*KABOOM!*

 The most famous of these was Mount Vesuvius. You may have heard of it. It's near Naples, Italy. Vesuvius had been sleeping for centuries, and then it suddenly "woke up" in the year AD 79. It must have been in a really bad mood. One and a half million tons per second of stones, ash, and fumes shot into the sky.

In seconds, the Roman cities of Pompeii and Herculaneum were buried under broiling ash, along with everyone who didn't get out in time. Sixteen thousand people died.

 The weird thing about Pompeii was it was buried so deep that nobody found it for about fifteen hundred years. Then, when it was discovered and unearthed, it was like a snapshot of life during the time of the Roman Empire. The victims were found in the exact positions they were in when they died, often with terrified looks on their faces. Weird!

 Vesuvius has erupted lots of times since the big one and as recently as 1944. It's the only volcano on the European mainland to erupt in the last hundred years. It's also considered to be one of the most dangerous volcanoes in the world today, because three million people live nearby. It could blow at any time.

Hurricanes

Quick: What's the difference between a hurricane, a cyclone, and a typhoon?

Give up?

There is no difference! It was a trick question. So nah-nah-nah boo-boo on you.

All those storms are the same thing. They're called hurricanes in the Atlantic and northeastern Pacific Ocean, they're called cyclones in the South Pacific and the Indian Ocean, and they're called typhoons in the northwestern Pacific. If you ask me, they should all be called the same thing: hurricanes.

Hurricanes are usually described by how fast they move. A category 1 hurricane moves 74 to 95 miles per hour. Not so bad.

A category 2 hurricane moves 96 to 110 miles per hour. You'd better hold on to your hat for one of those.

A category 3 hurricane moves 111 to 129 miles per hour. That's some serious wind.

A category 4 hurricane moves 130 to 156 miles per hour. You'd better look for another place to be.

And finally, a category 5 hurricane is the worst of all. It moves more than 157 miles per hour. Don't bother going home, because your house won't be there anymore.

The deadliest hurricane to hit the United States was the Great Galveston Hurricane of 1900 on the Texas coast. It was so deadly because back then there was no early warning system for hurricanes. Between six thousand and twelve thousand people died.

In 2005, Hurricane Katrina devastated the area around New Orleans and took at least fifteen hundred lives. Katrina first landed in Florida and dropped ten to fifteen inches of rain. Then it crossed the Gulf of Mexico, growing stronger and stronger. By the time it hit the Mississippi coast, storm surge waves were as high as twenty-eight feet. That's taller than a two-story house!

Once they start moving over land, hurricanes begin to slow down. Eventually, they blow themselves out.

New Orleans's famous Bourbon Street and the aftermath of Hurricane Katrina

A long time ago, hurricanes were named after saints: Santa Ana, San Felipe, and so on. During World War II, scientists started using women's names to describe hurricanes. That came to an end in 1978 when they started to use both men's *and* women's names.

Tornadoes

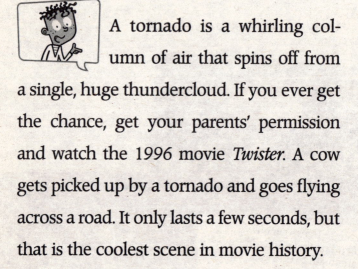 A tornado is a whirling column of air that spins off from a single, huge thundercloud. If you ever get the chance, get your parents' permission and watch the 1996 movie *Twister*. A cow gets picked up by a tornado and goes flying across a road. It only lasts a few seconds, but that is the coolest scene in movie history.

Sometimes tornadoes hop around, completely destroying one house and leaving the house right next door to it untouched.

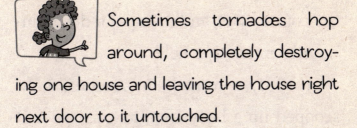

Tornadoes can have winds as fast as three hundred miles per hour. How fast is that? I'll tell you how fast it is. . . .

In 1931, a tornado in Mississippi picked up an eighty-three-ton train and threw it eighty feet.

A tornado in Oklahoma destroyed a motel, and after it was over somebody found the motel sign in Arkansas.

Another tornado in Oklahoma sucked up a small herd of cattle, carried it across the countryside, and then put it down unharmed in another field.

In 1981, a tornado in Ancona, Italy, scooped up a baby from its carriage and set it down unharmed on the ground.

In 1928, a tornado in Kansas plucked the feathers off chickens!

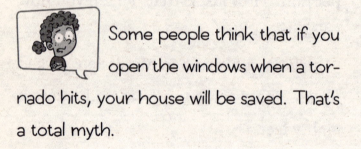
Some people think that if you open the windows when a tornado hits, your house will be saved. That's a total myth.

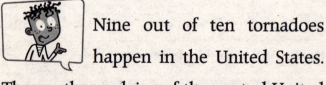
Nine out of ten tornadoes happen in the United States. The southern plains of the central United States have so many tornadoes that the

area is called Tornado Alley. It stretches from central Texas to northern Iowa, and from central Kansas and Nebraska east to western Ohio.

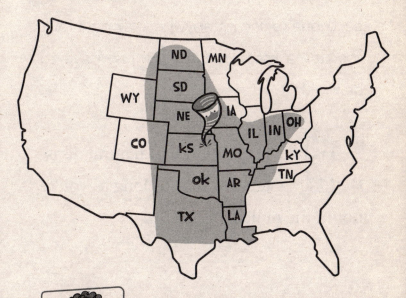

But *every* part of the world has been hit by some kind of natural disaster. You don't want to live near an active volcano, of course. Coastal areas have to deal with tropical storms and tsunamis. If you go inland, there are tornadoes, blizzards, dust storms, and thunderstorms to worry about. And an earthquake can hit anywhere along a fault line. It's a mess. I guess we just have to deal with it.

 I still think that natural disasters are cool, as long as you're not in the middle of one.

The Ending

We'll leave you with one last weird fast fact about geography. In the Philippines, close to Manila, there's this little island in the middle of a lake. The lake is on another island. And that island is in another lake. And that lake is on another island.

Maybe I'd better explain.

First, there are the Philippines, which

is a string of more than seven thousand islands in the Pacific Ocean. The largest island in the Philippines is called Luzon. On Luzon is a lake known as Lake Taal. Within that lake is an island, which is actually a volcano. It's called Volcano Island, so it has the perfect name.

Following me so far?

Okay, in the middle of Volcano Island is another lake, called Main Crater Lake. And guess what's in the middle of Main Crater Lake?

Another island! It's called Vulcan Point.

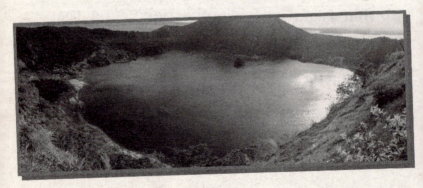

So there's an island in a lake on an island in a lake on an island in the ocean.

To make a long story short, geography is weird.

Congratulations! You reached the end of the book. See? That wasn't so boring, was it? You just learned about a million hundred weird fast facts about geography. So now you know *all* there is to know.

Wait, Arlo! There's more!

WHAT?! More?

There are a lot of facts about geography in this book. But we only had 167 pages. There wasn't room for *all* the weird facts in the world. If you want to see more of them, you should go to your school library or the public library. All you have to do is look for number 910–919 on the shelves. That's the part of the Dewey Decimal System where you'll find books about geography.

Books?! The library?! Are you nuts? Books are boring. And the library is the most boring place in the history of the world. I'd rather stay home.

You can even find weird fast facts about geography at home, Arlo! Just go to a computer and search for "weird facts about geography." Or "volcanoes." Or "mountains." Or *anything*! You could look up weird facts about doorknobs if you wanted to.

Here, I'll do it for you—brass doorknobs kill germs. It's true! Some metals, like brass, copper, aluminum, iron, lead, and silver, are known to kill bacteria and other microorganisms. I never would have known that if I hadn't looked it up on my computer.

Your *face* looks like a doorknob.

Very funny, Arlo. Anyway, you should poke around. It's fun! There's lots of cool information on the internet. All you have to do is look for it. You never know what you might find.

The best part about looking things up is that grown-ups are really impressed when you tell them stuff they don't know. If you take just about any fast fact in this book and tell it to your mom or dad, they probably will be hearing it for the first time. It will blow their minds! You see, grown-ups think kids are a bunch of dumbheads who don't know anything. But they're wrong!

So prove it and learn lots of new fast facts on your own. Maybe, if you work really hard at it, someday you'll know as many fast facts as Arlo and me.

 But it won't be easy!

GET A BRAIN FULL OF WEIRD FACTS FROM MY WEIRD SCHOOL!

Visit the World of Dan Gutman for online games, quizzes, and printable activities, plus a recap video of the entire My Weird School series!
www.booksandgames.com/dangutman

HARPER
An Imprint of HarperCollinsPublishers

www.harpercollinschildrens.com